JUST PASSIN' THRU

T C Carter

Cushing Publishing
www.cushingpublishing.com

Cushing Publishing

P.O. Box 38

Middlesex, NC 27557

This book is dedicated, with all my love, to my family.

Table of Contents

EMPTY BOXCARS

Sitting near the tracks alone
the horseback man gazes on,
watching that old train go by,
the midnight run to Omaha.

Empty boxcars, linked together,
doors stand open to the weather,
full moon blinks behind the train
going across Nebraska plains.

The engine howls it's traveling song,
empty boxcars trail along
swaying on the turning wheels
that polish tracks of solid steel.

The train must stretch a mile or more;
empty boxcars, open doors,
but the cowboy sitting on his mount
doesn't bother with a count.

The train has not been his friend,
it brought his trail days to an end,
so empty boxcars, open doors,
he wished that he would see no more.

DREAMED OF HORSES

I dreamed of horses
 Dreamed of men
That I would never see ag'in

 Except through cracks
In space and time
 That softly occupy my mind

As I lie in peaceful sleep
 I see them as they were back then
Those mighty horses, stalwart men

 That beckon me from shadowed land
To mount and gather there beside
 My friends on one more late night ride

The horsehair, smooth and soft and sleek
 I feel his heartbeat through my knees
His breath comes to me on the breeze

Familiar as the sky above
 It smells of oats and summer grass
And life we shared in long gone past

 Those boys and I restored to youth
We came from places near and far
 As if guided by some western star

We ride across the bluegrass prairies
 We see no train tracks, see no fences
We stop and loosen up our cinches

Beneath cottonwoods by a stream
 Where our horses drink and rest

T C CARTER

And we cowboys smoke and laugh and jest

We gather up refreshed once more
    The wind blows gentle through the trees
We mount ag'in upon our steeds

    And disappear into the mist
Flesh and blood now earth and grass
    And dreams and memories that last

The daylight comes to banish dreams
    Oh, if I had some Godly power
I would linger there uncounted hours

    But I awake back to the world
Having dreamed of horses, dreamed of men
    That I would never see ag'in

Except through cracks
    In space and time
That softly occupy my mind

HIS LAST RODEO

Little story 'bout Wade Pendleton
Born July twenty-seventh,
Nineteen twenty-nine
Deceased New Year's Day,
Nineteen hunnert and seventy-five
Cause of death....undetermined
    And it's called:

        "HIS LAST RODEO"

At forty-five and countin'
He could feel the years a'mountin'
He'd had collarbones and legs and arms
Broken, bruised and brought to harm

Too many times he had been hurt
When he was bucked onto the dirt
Too many times not in the money
Riding's fun, but it ain't funny

The stock seemed bigger, faster, meaner
And the grass was looking greener
Up there in the stands
Where they seat the paying fans

His cousin offered him some work
In his general store, some kind of clerk
But to him a job just don't mean jack
Unless it's done from a horse's back

He married once, married well
To a young, west Texas southern belle
Ah, she stuck like glue while he was winning
But later on stopped laughing, loving, grinning

10

T C CARTER

One day just up and tossed it in
Said she was moving on, leaving him
Packed up her stuff and out the door
...He never saw her anymore

Just another mile on the downhill ride
When strength and talent start to slide
But ya have t' stick with the thing ya know
And what he knew best was the rodeo

The best of times was in his twenties
Riding strong and winning plenty
Eating good and living fast
And paying bills with greenback cash

Now his meals were not so grand
Most times he had no cash in hand
Or just enough for an entry fee
He needed the ride, but it wasn't free

Funny how a wild eight second ride
Can fill a man with so much pride
And keep him coming back for more
Flush one day, the next one poor

But seasons came and seasons went
And he was feeling pert' near spent
The wins came now in short supply
But still he rode, still he tried

Some days were good, but most were bad
But, hell, no use in feeling sad
This life is what he chose to do
He was man enough to see it through

But he was drinking too much likker

JUST PASSIN' THRU

Was concerned about his ticker
Had no cash fer doctor bills
Was living life on hurtin' pills

He'd left his pick-up down at Donner Pass
That good old truck had breathed its last
Caught a ride with a trucking man
Who shared his meal of cheese and ham

He got entered in here at Bakersfield
With little left but guts and will
Hoping fer a lucky draw
He'd need to get a rough outlaw

If he had a hope to make a show
And maybe win a little dough
He was due to earn some pay
Maybe this would be the day

Now someday soon he'll see the end
When no longer he can ride ag'in
And I would be the first to say
He was good back in his day

But now he's played out his string
And, boys, it's just an awful thing
But I guess most of ya' know
This is prob'ly....his last rodeo

MONTANA SKY

Oh, that sky, Montana sky,
that stretches far beyond the eye,
that holds the bowl of stars in place
and paints its beauty on my face.

I wonder, God, if it will be,
when measured by eternity,
always that same Montana sky,
that stretches far beyond the eye,

that makes the lofty mountains glow
by light reflected from the snow,
while on prairies here below
there are things we'll never know.

Why does the sky look bigger here
than sky that's found most anywhere?
Oh, that sky, Montana sky,
that stretches far beyond the eye.

I wish I could have seen its birth
when God created all the earth
and sprinkled diamonds from his eye
and called it sky, Montana sky.

MORNING ON THE PRAIRIE

And in the morning I was waiting
for the sun to warm my face
and stretch my shadow 'cross the prairie
to another time another place

Where the haze above a cow camp
looked like gold dust in the sky
where horse hoof would be falling
and leaving time be drawing nigh

As the cowboys pulled their cinches
the trail boss gave his shout
like a trumpet call on judgement day
"Mount up boys....move 'em out"

It was cowboys in the saddle
with open country all the way
to the railheads waiting yonder
where the cowboys drew their pay

I'd like to cross just one more river
like to ride just one more mile
moving cattle 'cross the prairie
for just a little while

And relive how it used to be
before the fences came
and the farmers with their families
and the tracks that brought the trains

It was a hard life to be sure
but I never knew a cowpunch friend
who thought that he could work a job
with other kinds of men

T C CARTER

The cowboy breed was always different
free men born to wander far
their roots were loosely planted
their eyes upon the stars

And now the sun came breaking
from the earth up to the sky
God's campfire in the heavens
reflected in my eyes

And I thought I heard the lowing
of cattle drifting on the wind
and the jolly prattle flowing
of some long gone cowboy friends

I closed my eyes and drifted
as the morning sun warmed my face
and stretched my shadow 'cross the prairie
to another time another place

RODEO

I been busted up and broken up
And twisted half in two
Sometimes I wonder if I'm smart
To do the things I do

But rodeo is all I know
And eatin' dirt comes with the deal
But there ain't much way to make a dime
While I lay around and heal

So I braid some reins and mend some tack
And count the days 'till I get back
To where the living is risky
And the broncos are frisky

And the eight second clock
Ticks in my head
And counts down the time
'Till this cowboy is dead

TEXAS RANGER IRA BLUES

This feller was a tall man
He stood 'bout six-foot two
He weighted one hundred eighty-five
And his eyes were cobalt blue

He had wandered down to Houston
Five months short of twenty-two
Took an oath and got a badge
And so began the legend
Of Texas Ranger Ira Blues

He had come up in a hard life
Busting sod behind a plow
Pulled by a mule called Nellie
Where Ira Blues made a vow

That he would not spend his life
Scratching out a little living
From the ground beneath his feet
That took more than it was giving

But soon enough he went to war
Where he served the southern states
And when it came down to the end
He began to contemplate

On what he'd make of several skills
That seemed to be just nature's way
Formed somehow in his mother's womb
Before he saw the light of day

He could track a rabbit over rock
And his aim was always true
He strived to ever do the right thing

17

JUST PASSIN' THRU

According to the good book
And the law, and Ira Blues

So Texas Rangers seemed his calling
To help tame the lawless west
Where he could put his skills and talents
To the lawman's rigid test

His first assignment sent him south
To a dusty border town
Where he found a vicious killer
And was forced to put him down

And this was just the first
Of many outlaws he would seek
To bring to justice for their crimes
Against the honest and the meek

Some he brought before a judge
Some refused to go without a fight
But one way or the other
Ira Blues would set things right

The years passed by quickly
And his reputation spread and grew
And the bad men there in Texas
Lived in fear of Ira Blues

Then one year he turned his badge in
And said so long to all his friends
And the Texas Ranger legend
Of Ira Blues came to an end

Nobody knows why it happened
And they never heard further news
But Texans love the legend
Of Texas Ranger Ira Blues

CHANGE THAT AIN'T WORKING

I'm too old to think
that I could be
some other feller
that ain't me.
I tried to change
my stubborn ways,
and pay more heed
to how I graze,
fixing up my teeth
real straight,
was told I ought
to contemplate
some other way
to fix my hair,
and wear my clothes
so they compare
to some cowboy
up on the screen,
a feller that
I've never seen,
and now it's got me
feeling mean.
I'm going back
to my old rags,
festooned with
Sears and Roebuck tags,
casting off
the tooth appliance,
and trust again
to the science,
of nature running wild
…I'll be as stubborn
as a child,
let my hair

JUST PASSIN' THRU

look like a wreck,
growing long
all down my neck,
and my grub

will change ag'in
to what it use'ta
be back then
when I was living
old and free,
with the feller
that was me.
So, if how I am
don't satisfy
I'll never try
to rectify,
or change the way
I live at home
'cause who cares?
I live alone.

THE SWEET GRASS HILLS

The stone tilts toward
                    the west
wearing the marks of time
                    and seasons

Alone it stands in the
                    Sweet Grass Hills
a faithful sentinel
                    at its post

Black scales and moss obscure
                    life span and name
of he who sleeps in the earth
                    to dust returned

and the wind that bends
                    the Sweet Grass
whispers his name
                    to God alone

BUSTED

He come up from the west Texas country;
the bank took his ranch
and his old dog had died,
all he had left was his horse and his saddle
and his lucky gold peso,
and what was left of his pride.

But the peso hadn't brought him no luck,
and the sky hadn't brought him much rain,
and the banker was wanting his money
and the cowboy was feeling the pain.

His cattle rode the train to the Ft. Worth Stockyards
and was sold to the high bidder there,
but the money was owed to the banker
and nobody but the cowboy had cared.

It was the drought that had beat out the life
of all his hard work and his sweat
mother nature had done her dang level best,
to keep the cowboy from winning a good ranchers bet.

So, he come up from the west Texas country
hoping for a change in the way his luck run;
found a job on a spread in Montana
far from the heat of that hot Texas sun.

He found an old dog, he was all skin and bones
and looked like his times had been tough,
so he fixed him a bed in little used shed
and made sure he was fed quite enough.

Yes, he come up from the west Texas country,
busted and needing a new start,

and a Montana rancher hired him for wages
doing work that was stamped in his heart.

When he rode up from the west Texas country,
got that new job and another old mutt,
he never did deal with another slick banker,
but the peso of gold was kept for good luck.

CYCLE

They came from the hills
And the farms and the mills
And followed the calling
That pointed them west

Where they worked for short pay
And rode herd for long days
And studied the trail ways
To prove up to be best

And some of them fell
On the old cattle trails
Driving herds to the north
To be shipped to the east

And the trail friends they had
Would be grieved and be sad
As they laid in the ground
A cowboy deceased

With the boys gathered 'round
Someone said he found
That this boy was a good 'un
From the day of his birth

The cow boss said a word
And a short prayer was heard
And the cowboy was covered
With a blanket of earth

The markers they made
Would wear down and fade
And the names would return
To the breast of the earth

And the grass that would grow
Above the cowboys below
Would be nurtured
By men of intrinsic worth

And the winds that would blow
Where the tall Bluestem grows
Would sweep the souls
Of the men to the sky

Where the God of them all
Was standing there tall
A thousand hills covered with cattle
And cowboys the apple of His eye

LAST SUNSET

At a saloon down in San Antone
he stood at the bar all alone,
one boot heel hooked atop the rail
he thought of days out on the trail

He'd hoped that he would run into
some cowboys, maybe one or two
who had ridden by his side
on one of those long cattle drives

But some had lost the war with age
and left behind this earthly stage,
some had gone to other climes
changing with the changing times

Some had took up other trades
that didn't suit how they were made,
a few he heard were on the run
for being foolish with a gun

But he was set in simple ways
and how he'd lived in cow trail days.
The new ways taking over now
did not seem right to him somehow

And so he finished up his beer;
it looked like he'd be staying here.
He'd try for work on some small spread
where he could earn his daily bread

A bunkhouse cowboy tending cows,
he'd do the best that he knew how
and when he sees his last sunset
he will be a cowboy yet

HORSES TO START

My boys both think
Maybe I should move to town
They brought it up to me
Last time they come around

Now I've never been a town man
Been a cowboy all my days
It's just too late in the game of life
For me to change my ways

But I told 'em I would
Think on it
And I did
For just a little bit

But I got horses to start
And fences to mend
And things I've done before
That need doing a'gin

Their Momma suddenly
Passed away
A year ago
Come the tenth of May

I reckon they think
Their Pa needs some tending
And there ain't no use
In me pretending

That I ain't hurtin'
And lonesome too
Thinking 'bout the life
That we both knew

JUST PASSIN' THRU

But town won't fix what's broke
And time won't cure the pain
Staying home is what I need
To keep me mostly sane
'Cause work is where I find
The most relief
From the never-ending
Heavy weight of grief

And like I said before
I got horses that I need to start
They're coming up on four years' old
Good horses, strong and smart

Proper age I think
To get 'em started right
And spending days with them
Helps me make it through the night

So I cain't move to town
And I'm sure my boys know
That as long as I'm my own man
There's no way that I would go

'Cause I got horses to start
And fences to mend
And things I've done before
That need doing a'gin

OLD SADDLE

The saddle that he cinched up
On the Morgan every day
Was looking kinda frazzled
It had seen some better days

He had thought about a new one
The cat'logs had 'em by the score
And they had about a dozen
Down at Big Al's general store

He thought 'em mighty pretty
Some were fancy some were plain
But he always thought he'd wait awhile
Then look at them again

But when he swung up on the Morgan
That old saddle felt right good
And he wondered if another rig
Would fit him like it should

This 'un wasn't gold durn fancy
Didn't have no silver trim
It was made fer working cattle
And that was good enough fer him

Then he thought about the Morgan
How a change would set with him
'Cause this old ragged saddle
Fit like natural grown on skin

Well sir, that was the thing what won the day
The Morgan's vote was all it took
To forget about new saddles
And throw away the cat'log book

BUCK RAMSEY REMEMBERED

Buck Ramsey from his wheelchair
Reached deep into his soul
He knew the cowboy lingo
Knew the cowboy life
And those thoughts of which
He did so grandly write
Keep me up late into the night
Memorizing, reading, somehow needing
To absorb the treasure
Written from his heart

To share his love of the cowboy life
And maybe even some small part
Of the loss that churned through his veins
His constant ache
His bit shank broke as he rode Cinnamon
Through the breaks

And there in one bad stroke of luck
He came unglued, he landed wrong
His back was broke
And in a flash Buck Ramsey feared
His riding days had disappeared

What thoughts he had I cannot say
But pain and fear assaulted him
Where he lay
They found him lying quiet and still
And on a travoi sling
They pulled him up
From where he had spilled

They flew him out on a helicopter
And turned him over to a team of doctors

T C CARTER

Who did what had to be done
Did all they could for this dear son

You'll never walk or ride again
They said
He thought in that bleak moment
It would be better
to be dead

The cowboy life was what he knew
And he was one, good and true
The thought of life
In a wheelchair cage
Filled his eyes with bitter tears
And his heart with
Burning rage

He drank...to forget
And dull the aching pain
Of knowing he would never ride again

For twenty years or so he drifted
In the grip of alcoholic haze
It seemed his life was lived for naught
And there was no hope
For what he sought
This was his burden night and day

But he had always read
Had, in fact, learned to write
In a two room school at Middlewell
With four grades to a room
As a student, he did not excel

His gift, his ear for language
Came from the rhythm of old-time gospel hymns
And Baptist preachers

JUST PASSIN' THRU

And writers from Shakespeare to Pushkin
These, and others, were his teachers

And so he wrote
As a journalist
And a free-lance writer
Buck Ramsey would never climb the windmill
But he would always be a fighter

He learned to play the guitar
And wrote his cowboy poetry still
He was a true student of the world of words
And his writings begged to be heard

At a cowboy poets gathering
Somewhere along the line
He discovered kindred spirits
Keeping the cowboy flame alive
Singers and poets of the cowboy way
And his long dark night
Yielded
To the light of day

There was no way to know
He had less than two decades to live
But those would not be lived in fear

He would play his music
Sing his songs
Recite the poems he wrote
For just as long
As breath would fill his lungs
Until his life was swept away
The last poem had not been read
The last song had not been sung

His reputation spread and grew

T C CARTER

As he wrote of things he knew
And his sweet spirit made him friends
That would stick with him to the end

Even at high noon
Or under full bright moon
The shadow of his gift fell deep and wide
Where all the cowboy tribe
Came to recognize
He was the north star of cowboy writers
Cowpunchers and wild horse fighters

From his horse wreck in the river breaks
To his White House invitation
Buck Ramsey's heart, though battered
Never lost its gentle nature
And this: it should come as no surprise
His soul was showing in his eyes

Six days short of sixty
Sitting upright in his chair
Reading from the book
Of Ecclesiastes
His gentle heart, beat its last note
As he read what the preacher wrote:

"To everything there is a season,
and a time to every purpose
under the heaven:
A time to be born,
and a time to die;
a time to plant,
and a time to pluck up
that which is planted;
A time to kill, and a time to heal;
a time to break down,
and a time to build;

JUST PASSIN' THRU

A time to weep, and a time to laugh;
a time to mourn, and a time to dance."
    (Eccl. 3: 1-3)

He died on a cold January day
And Buck's ashes were put away
Until the springtime of wildflowers
And bluestem grass
And sunshine
When cowpunch friends
Would combine
Their send-offs at a spot Buck would know
Somewhere on the river breaks
Of the Llano Estacado

J. B. Allen recited Buck's classic poem
"Anthem"
From memory
As his ashes were set free
Among his cowboy friends
And now he rides ag'in
Unfettered
On the wind

COWBOY AND HIS DOG

Stopped in at the vet's office
this morning
to pick up a case of dog food.
Grizzled old cowboy sitting
on a bench
with his dog lying
on the floor.
Pretty dog,
medium size,
long light brown hair.
Cowboy was skinny
as a rail,
elbows on his knees
looking down at his dog.
He had jeans on
stuck down in a pair
of ragged boots,
well-worn blue work shirt
and a straw cowboy hat
that had seen some
hard use.
Sporting about
a week worth of stubble
and a thick grey mustache
hiding his top lip,
he was about as cowboy
as cowboy gets.
While I was waiting
for the girl to get my order,
I sez to him,
"Your dog okay?"
He turns his face up to me,
but didn't say anything,
so I sez, "Just got him in

JUST PASSIN' THRU

for shots?"
He kind 'a nodded
and said,
"He's my buddy,"
and I replied,
"Well, ya couldn't have
a better one."
Then he lifted his eyes
slightly,
a little melancholy smile
turned the corners
of his mouth up,
and he said,
"Onliest one I got,
most of the time."
About that time
the girl came out
with my order,
and someone else came
to talk to the cowboy,
so I paid up and left.
Coming home
I felt a little melancholy
myself.
I wished I could have talked
to the old cowboy more.
I hoped his buddy
would be okay,
I wished that I could
be his friend.

OLD CALLAHAN

Old Callahan,
that ranahan,
the kind cowboys admire
He built his brand
on grassy land,
and he never was for hire
Nobody thought
that he'd be caught
and convinced to settle down
But a little gal
got him corralled,
and now he's living in a town

*ranahan (refers to a top hand)

TEXAS

Early morning,
      gentle breeze,
   full moon
pierces the dark,

ocean of grass
      ripples the prairie,
   softly whispers
nature's words,

iron ribbon
      of tracks
   in the distance
follows the river,

train whistle
      sings its song,
   smoke tracing
a trail to Dallas,

morning prayer,
      small fire,
   hot coffee,
horse grazing.

Startin' right,
      just me and him,
   and Texas,
early morning.

Beulah Geneva Carter and TC Carter
(photo courtesy of TC Carter)

NOBODY GETS TO BE A COWBOY FOREVER

Mama said,"nobody
gets to be a cowboy forever"

It's the only thing
she ever told me
that wasn't true
but she thought it was true
so it don't count none against her

That's me and her
in the photograph
I'm about five years old I reckon
holding on to Mama's hand
eyes turned down to the ground
all shy and innocent looking

Got my little cowboy outfit on
matching chaps and vest
with a plaid shirt
I expect Mama bought it at
Woolworth's

She lived to be ninety-six
but she's a pretty young woman
in the photograph

Daddy wasn't there for the picture
not home from the war yet
He never did come all the way home
Alcohol killed him
when he was fifty-five

Aww, they'd get a chuckle
to see me now

T C CARTER

still cowboying
skinny as a fence post
and gray as Methuselah's beard
but still pulling my own weight
at a cow camp

Don't know how to do nothing else
and ain't about to start learning now
Way I figger it
long as there's cows
there'll be cowboys

Mama said, nobody
gets to be a cowboy forever
and she believed it
but it wasn't true

HEAVEN BOUND

When the end of yer life's at the door,
and ya find ya ain't breathing no more,
ya just needs ta relax
'cause ya ain't comin' back,
and ya know it right down to ya core.

Ya won't be needing them chaps and riata,
the spurs and hat can be left on the peg,
and yer horse is at ease in the pasture,
sun on his back, and up on three legs.

So, as ya go, on yer way up ta heaven
don't try to stop off and chat,
or try in yer head ta figger,
exactly, or close, where yer at.

Yer tickets got a one-way
blood-colored stamp,
thar's angels leading up the way,
and the pearly gates are wide open
ta welcome ya home where yul stay.

THE HAIRCUT

Me and Skinny Butler
rode into town yestiddy
to git a wagon load of supplies

While the storekeep
was filling the order
me and Skinny
ambled over to the saloon
fer a little dust cutter
and whatever news
we could pick up

Found out
there was a new barber
in town
fresh arrived from
somewhar in Missouri
so I decided to treat myself
to a boughten haircut

Hadn't set foot in a real
barber shop
in four or five years

Now this barber
was a young man
sort of a nervous twitchy
type 'a feller
but he had a paper
on the wall
that said he was a
bonafide graduate
of a haircutttin' school
so I set myself down

JUST PASSIN' THRU

in the barber chair
and he cinched his cloth
up around my neck
and co-minced to cut hair

Now, I ain't known t' be
real picky or t' be a complainer
and I didn't want t' discourage
a young feller
just startin' out
but I shore thought two bits
was a mighty high price
to pay
fer the scalping I took

Back in seventy-two
I had a one-eyed buffalo skinner
cut my hair with a Bowie knife
that done a better job
than this 'un
and he didn't charge me
no two bits neither

Lesson learned I reckon

GOING HOME

If you happen to see an old man
Come a'riding up your way
And he rides up slow and easy
On a horse of dappled gray

Sittin' his saddle cowboy proud
Like a gentleman at his ease
His chaps showing years of use
And worn thin about the knees

A silverbelly hat stained dark
From time and sweat and sun and dust
His boots needin' heels and half soles
And Texas spurs dark with rust

His vest has seen some better days
And the shirt wears a patch or two
His skin dark and weathered
Hooded eyes of greenish blue

And if you think that he's a throwback
To a time already past
You'd be mostly right I reckon
But times and seasons never last

If you offer him some vittels
And some oats for his gray
He will kneel down on his knees
And there begin to pray

He'll ask the Lord to bless you
For your kindness and the cooking
That will help him down that long old trail
To keep on with his looking

JUST PASSIN' THRU

For a place where he can fit in
And do the work he's always done
With other cowboy riders
On the downside of the sun
He won't ask much for himself
His prayer will be for you
That you'll have good health and fortune
In everything you say and do

He won't overstay his welcome
You might not want this man to leave
But he hasn't found his home yet
And he'll say that he believes

That it's just beyond his eyesight
And in that rich and fertile land
There's a ranch that he's been promised
Not made by human hands

And when he leaves you won't forget him
He'll find a place there in your mind
And leave a yearning in your heart
For that home you'll want to find

WILD HORSES

I rode with the wild horses,
we rode like the wind,
oh, I wish I could ride
with those Mustangs again

They were free on the prairie,
no man had a claim
on the free-roaming horses
with wind in their manes

The thunder in their hooves
beat a song in my chest;
when I rode with wild horses
I rode with the best

SEND OFF

I dreamed last night that I had died
A peaceful look was on my face
But there was no mistake about it
I had crossed the finish line of my earthly race

The boys was looking sad and somber
I thought, I know just how you feel
'Cause I've been there beside you
When other men died along the trail

But everybody has to die... someplace
What better place than the cowboy's church
With mountain walls and blue-sky roof
Doing work I love to do with men I love this much

They've been my family, been my friends
Saved my life a time or two
And now they bear me to the earth
Since my time down here was through

Cook had washed dust from off my face
My hands was laid acros't my chest
My hair was combed, my clothes was brushed
I was fixed up to my best

They wrapped me in my bed gear
With the gentle touch of roughhewn hands
And laid me in my resting place
In a little sunbaked spot of Oklahoma land

Boss said these words over me
Lord, we've lost a top cowhand today
But our loss will tally to your gain
I reckon it's always been that way

T C CARTER

He said, boys, we're gonna miss T.C.
And he wouldn't fault us none fer leaving
But we got a herd to get up north
So we'll have to trail 'em while we're grieving

So they swung into their saddles
And rode sadly on their way
Men with work still to do
In another eighteen-hour day

Then I woke up from my dream
I smelled cook's coffee on the fire
So I sprung up and poured a cup
My spirits was never higher

'Cause here I got another day
To live and love the life I'm given
Cherished now more than ever
Oh, it's a grand day to be living

Now, I've pondered some on that dream
And how it's worked on me
I never put no stock in dreams
But I think this 'un helped me see

That every day belongs to God
Every friend a priceless treasure
Every trail we get to ride
A gift beyond our measure

Well, I'm glad it was just a dream
But I hope it works out just that way
When I cross the great divide
And leave behind my earth-bound days

It was the kind of send off

JUST PASSIN' THRU

A cowboy wants from cowboy friends
The boys had done the best they could
And said a heartfelt adios and a soft amen

LETTER TO SIS

Dear Sis,

I thought I might come see you this spring
When the trees start to bud and the flowers start to bloom
I sure would like to see you again
If you can tolerate this old cowboy taking up room

If I have my druthers I won't be no particular bother at night
I'll bring my bedroll along and sleep out under the stars
If it won't scandalize your neighbors too much or give 'em a fright
In fair weather I never did cotton to bunking under shelter

I like to stretch out
Where there ain't nothing between me and my maker
'Cept fer a sky full of what He put up there
You know, Sis, I never did have much schooling or churching
So, I figger you'll think me and the Lord to be a peculiar pair

But He has helped me t' mend my ways…considerable
Don't cuss near what I used to do; Oh, I'll still take a drink or two
But I ain't been what you might call drunk fer nigh on to a year or so
Today was payday; some of the boys went to town but I decided…
I wouldn't go

Recon I must be gettin' old; been stomped on too many times
By cattle and horses….sometimes by men

JUST PASSIN' THRU

I could always be knocked down, ya know,
But I could never be kept down
Too much pride in my character,
 But I hope it ain't enough to make it a sin

One time or t'other I've cowboyed from Montana down to
Texas
Rough-necked once up in the Oklahoma oil patch,
Didn't like it; moved around at lot, like most cowboys do
Seems like we git a itch, we just gotta give it a scratch

But I'm headin' into my third year here on Mr. Will
Johnson's spread
He's a good man and fair to a fault and I've always said
He treats horses right and men better 'n most of us
deserve
I'm thinking 'bout settling down here if he'll have me
I reckon I'd be coming out of Dallas on the train
It's a long ways from here to Baltimore
And I ain't never bucked out one them contraptions before
If I was still a young man I'd come on horseback

But the boys will see to my horse and saddle
And what little bit of plunder I got
They say a rolling stone don't gather no moss
And I reckon that's right 'cause I sure don't have a lot

But I will say this, Sis, I don't have many regrets neither
Not much I'd want to change about my life
'Less'n it'd be that time I got shot down in El Paso....
But that made me a believer.....so reckon I'd leave that
alone too

Well now, Sis,
You give John and the rest of your family my best regards
And if the good Lord don't call my number and the creek
don't rise

T C CARTER

I'll see you later on in the springtime
And we'll do a little bit'a catching up.. on our lives

Your loving brother,
T.C. Carter
29 December 19 hunnard and ought 3

HEAVEN AT THE RIMROCK

As he sat up on that rimrock,
and watched the sun
wake up the sky,
he thought a piece of heaven
had settled in his eyes.

This must be the way
creation looked
when it was first day new,
untouched by human hand,
and a-sparkling with the dew

He thought,
if I should die up on this rimrock,
the Lord must surely know,
this valley looks like heaven must,
so I would not have too far to go.

NO WAGES

Feller offered me a job yesterday,
some kinda Earl, what he said;
come over from jolly old England
and bought him a west Texas spread.

I don't know what a Earl does fer wages,
but he talks about it in pounds;
he likes to show off all of his do-dads,
and spread his importance around.

He lives in a place up in Denver,
twelve bedrooms and a garden of flowers;
our little place would fit in his kitchen,
but it's all that we need and it's ours.

He bought the ranch for a place he could play,
bring his friends down to impress;
they'd ride around on some horses,
shoot guns, and generally, make a big mess

It sounds like the spread is a good one,
and the wages he offered was fair;
more money than I've seen in one piece,
maybe more money than we need to bear.

My Mary and me talked it over,
and we quickly come to agree;
we don't want to work for no wages,
we'd rather be poor and be free.

Well, the Earl didn't take it too kindly,
heard I was the best hand around,
but Mary and me wasn't looking for nothing;
what we wanted, we'd already found.

CIVILIZED

Boys, yul hafta turn yer guns in here,
before ya goes ta sloshing rotgut beer,
and a-punching holes up in the sky.

I figger ya never realized
this town is a-gittin' civilized;
leastways that's what we aim to try.

Taking guns to the ball
don't mix too good with alcohol;
the crosses on boot hill can testify

Now, what goes up always comes down,
and hot lead rain don't work in town,
so hand them shooters over with no fuss

And now yul go and have yer fun
without shootin' off yer guns,
while I hold 'em at the jail in trust

That's jest the way it is these days,
yul git 'em back when ya ride away
a'whooping up a cloud a' dust.

THE LIFE AND LEGEND OF U.S. MARSHAL BASS REEVES

This feller was a tall man;
he stood 'bout six-foot two,
he weighed one hundred, eighty-five
and his aim was deadly true.

He was the first black U.S. Marshal
west of the Mississippi,
his horse stood at fourteen hands,
a Colt forty-five was on his hip.

But he was born into slavery
back in eighteen thirty-eight
on a hard-scrabble cattle ranch
before Texas was a state.

He had come up in a hard life,
his mama was his only guide;
she taught him that no matter what,
Son, never lose your pride.

No man is your true master,
this life is not your destiny,
the Lord has told me in a dream
that my son will soon be living free.

And so it came to pass:
young Bass fled for his life
on a Roman nose pony
with two guns and a knife.

Indian Territory became his refuge
though danger did abound,
for a black man with property

JUST PASSIN' THRU

was not often to be found.

Befriended by the Indians
when he saved a young girls life,
they offered him a home
and some say he found a wife.
For more than twenty years
he spent his life with the tribe;
he learned their survival skills
and knew the country far and wide.

But bad men congregated here;
that Indian country had no law,
so outlaws found a haven
though it was wild and raw.

Then a bloody war raged across the south;
and in eighteen, sixty-three
a proclamation by Mr. Lincoln
set black people free.

No longer considered a fugitive
Bass Reeves went to Arkansas
and built a life as a cattleman,
ten children called him Pa.

If this were all there was to tell
there is much we could commend,
but this is where the legend starts,
not where the story ends.

Congress appointed a federal judge
tough as the land he was sent to tame;
his nickname was the Hanging Judge,
Isaac Parker was his name.

Two hundred deputy federal marshals

T C CARTER

served as the judge's clean-up band
and fifty-one-year-old Bass Reeves
was one of the first to raise his hand.

He spoke the language of three tribes,
knew the country like a book,
could track a rabbit over rock,
had all it took to catch a crook.

Some think that Bass took the job
to help his Indian friends,
to stop the invading desperados
and bring their evil to an end.

More times than we can know
Bass rode out with warrant in hand,
and against all odds and expectations
he always got his man.

Fourteen came tied across a horse's back,
many more came with shackled hands
but one way or the other
Bass was cleaning up the land.

He even had to track down
and bring in one of his own sons;
he knew it was what he had to do,
but the hardest thing he'd ever done.

For thirty-two years he hunted men
who were the worst of humankind;
and the outlaws rode filled with fear
when Bass Reeves was on their mind.

But the territory had become mostly tamed
and Marshal Reeves had lead the way;
now it was time to step aside

59

JUST PASSIN' THRU

and settle down somewhere to stay.

In Muskogee, Oklahoma
he pinned on a constable's star,
but two years later Bright's disease
killed the man who had come so far.

Chief Marshal Leo Bennet said,
"He was the finest deputy I ever had;
he never shirked his duty
and he always made a stand."

Let history be what it is;
Bass Reeves lives there to this day,
life and legend, one blended voice,
listen to what it has to say.

END OF THE LINE

I think it's over
I've run my course
It's hard for me to ride a horse

I'll never build another fire
to boil my coffee
I'm not for hire

I'm too stove up
I'm too broke down
and I can't make my bed in town

But my pards will see me through
until the end
it's what we do

COWBOY X

Some cowboys come from ol' Virginny',
some from Kentuck' and Alabam';
went yonder way bound for Texas,
done with fighting Uncle Sam.

Some cowboys come from Carolina,
no place left to call their home,
walked their way into the sunset,
down to Texas they did roam.

They come from other places
round the country here and there;
they made their way all by themselves
or traveled there in pairs.

And much of what they learned in Texas
was the old vaquero ways,
all the skills of working cattle
that they would practice all their days.

Most had but meager learning
in the world of books and such,
and it might have mattered some, to some,
but it didn't matter much.

When he signed on to a trail drive
once he proved he had the bark
the trail boss never thought it strange
that he used an X to make his mark.

These boys was made of grit and gristle
with a spine of tempered steel;
they were used to all the hardship cards
that they were handed in the deal.

T C CARTER

Some lived the life for thirty years,
some died out on the trail;
and heaven now would fit them boys
much better than a seat in hell.

So, let me tip my hat, boys
to all the cowboys that I've known;
to those with frost upon their hair
and to them already gone.

And when we meet up yonder,
where the good Lord's cattle graze,
we'll find our X there in His book
and the record of our cowboy days.

TRAIN'S A'COMING

They say the train's a'coming soon
They're laying rails acros't the land
Coming like a cloud of locust
Chewing up the rock and sand

Cuttin' through the mountains
Dropping down the trees
Railroad tracks a'coming
Anywhere they dang well please

They cut acros't the Chisholm Trail
Without a thought or care
Whoever would have thunk it
Why, it's gall beyond compare

Don't they know about us cowpokes
That we're kings of open range
The potentates of hill and dale
Not wanting railroad change

Oh, sure, they've seen us ridin' herd
We've seen 'em gawk and stare
Then turn back to their section maps
And say, we'll run some rail right there

Wherever there's a dollar
Or a nickel to be made
That's where they'll send the black beast
That's where their hand is played

All around the campfires
Of the cowpokes on the plain
They heap derision on the steel tracks
And lament the coming of the train

T C CARTER

I'd like to shoot the belching beast
A forty-four right through its heart
Run it off a trestle high
And watch it crash and come apart

But that's just idle thoughts and such
There's no way to stop or slow
The great wild west intruder
Who wants to wander to and fro

And when they fill the land up
With sod busters and woolly sheep
Followers of the shiny rails
Claiming range land they can keep

Cowpokes will be the fellers
With nothing left to do but think
And reminisce and wonder
How their world changed in a blink

JUST PASSIN' THRU

A lone rider called out to the camp
The cowboys shouted, Come on in
They said, Have some bacon and beans, old man
The coffee's hot and strong as sin

He would tell these boys about his ramblin's
But first he ate his fill and drank a cup
Then he settled back and rolled a smoke
Popped a match and lit 'er up

He said, Boys, that was mighty fine
And I'm much obliged to you
Now I'll tell you what I've done and heard
As I've been passin' thru

My ramblin's took me thru the nations
Traded some with Cheyenne and the Sioux
They don't seem to mind a man
Long as he's just passin' thru

I've been all acros't the west, boys
And what I say, I think is true
The cowboy life is best reserved
For men just passin' thru

Well, you know how it goes, boys
When it comes to settlin' down
Our breed is made for ramblin'
Not nesting in some town

Now, I likes the ladies good as any
But every gal I ever knew
Was looking fer a settled man
And I was a man just passin' thru

T C CARTER

There's a heap of talk about a railroad
And they say the deal is almost done
Of where the tracks will cut the trail
And the trains will make their run

Boys, once they cut acros't the trails
It'll start gettin' hard on me and you
And all the men who drive these herds
Men just passin' thru

How long before our day is done
I wish that I could say I knew
But I'm just a man crossing the land
…I'm just passin' thru

But whatever we do in this short life
And this ain't nothing new
When it gits right down to the nubby truth
   We're all just passin' thru

CONQUISTADORS

There will come a time
When the rivers seem too wide to cross
And the hills too steep to climb

But we will cross the shallow streams
And climb the gentle hills
And remember better times

He's been my friend, my close companion
Never failed me in the clutch
And I hope that I have done for him
Just about as much

We rode the Judith's back one springtime
Early fall the Sierry Pete's
And saw the work of God's own hand
From the Colorado Peaks

We braved the waters of the Arkansas
The Powder, Platte, Canadian
The Trinity, the Brazos and the Rio Grande

So come what may and come what will
We've conquered rivers, conquered hills
Conquistadors of horizons lying west

But our reign is coming to its end
And still my horse is my best friend
And I'll always do for him what I think best

We've seen it all, lived life well
We've been kings without a crown
But there's one thing we'll never do
We'll never make our camp in town

A LITTLE RAIN

It's 1-0-2 outside a'gin,
chance of rain looks none to slim,
the critter coats are hot to touch,
cowboy hats, just as much;
not a drop of rain has fell
out on this dusty cattle trail
fer days, I've lost the count of it,
and I'm too dry to work up spit.
Ain't no trees fer miles around
to let some shade touch the ground,
the H20's in short supply,
nobody knows or figgers why,
but hold up boys, what's that there,
a little cloud up in the air,
all puffed up and looking proud,
let's hope it's followed by a crowd.
We know the Lord has got the stuff,
and all we want is just enough
to break the heat and settle dust
at least enough to make a crust.
It's not my nature to complain,
but, Lord, we need a little rain.

SCRATCHING THAT ITCH

I've 'et my share of arena dirt
when big bulls and wild broncs
bucked me down,
and my life has been saved
more than once I believe
by wild men rodeo clowns.

I know what it's like
to be flush with the cash
and I know how it is to be broke.
I've had steak on my plate
and all I could eat,
washed down with whiskey and Coke.

Then there's been times
when the pickings was slim
and my ribs was startin' to show,
but all I could do
was to stay on the road
and keep doing the things that I know.

I've showed up for work
in trucks new off the lot
and I've thumbed my way down the road,
but one way or t'other
I got there in time
to make the whole eight or get throwed.

I've had luck with the ladies
who think cowboys are cool,
and hang out at the rodeo grounds,
and I fell pretty hard for a couple of gals,
but romance on the road
ain't near good as it sounds.

T C CARTER

But that's how it goes
in this life that I chose;
it sure ain't no way to get rich,
but long as I'm here
on the green side of grass
I'll have to keep scratching that itch.

THE KILLING OF DORA HAND

Dora Hand had been a singer
Of grand opera in the east
A voice as pure as sunshine
That could have soothed a savage beast

Why she left it all behind her
Is anybody's guess
But by rail and coach she travelled
To her new home in the west

Dodge City, out in Kansas
Was where she chose to settle in
A cowtown at its zenith
Taking care of business with Texas cattlemen

Wyatt Earp was the marshal
Who always did what he had to do
And he had drawn a dead line
That split the town in two

The Alhambra Saloon and Gambling House
Was the first place Dora stopped
On the south side of the dead line
Dog Kelley hired her on the spot

She had a stunning beauty
That men and women all agreed
Whether she was saint or sinner
Was a rare and lovely sight to see

She was soon Queen of the Fairy Belles
Dodge City's name for dance hall girls
And she sang bawdy cowboy songs
In that rough edged, smoky world

T C CARTER

But by day dressed as a lady
Her deeds were known to one and all
Her response to others troubles
Was of the highest call

She crossed the dead line twice on Sundays
Dressed all in simple black
Lead the folks in singing church hymns
And listened to the preaching before she walked on back

Dog Kelley owned the Alhambra
Where Dora Hand plied her trade
He was also the city mayor
Known to have a hand in, where money could be made

But he handled young Jim Kennedy rough
And tossed him out one night
Jim swore that he would kill him
To even up the fight

In the act of a lowly coward
Just before the dawn had cracked
Jim shot five holes through the bedroom wall
Of Dog Kelley's two room shack

But he didn't know that Dora Hand and Fannie Garret
Had rented Kelley's shack
And when his bullets tore through the wall
One entered Dora's back

Jim was the son of Mifflin Kennedy
The partner of Richard King
They owned the biggest ranch in Texas
Their influence had some sting

But this was murder plain and simple

JUST PASSIN' THRU

And Wyatt set out to bring him in
The mayor said, Bring him back alive
All of Dodge will want to deal with him

Wyatt rode through an awful rainstorm
And caught his man this side of the Cimarron
The raging river stopped him
From being Texas gone

But the county claimed jurisdiction
And took young Jim in hand
Sent to Texas for his father
To come as quickly as he can

Well, ya know where the story's going
And I wish it wasn't so
But the county claimed there was no case
And Jim was free to go

And there for some Judas gold
Dora Hand was betrayed
And her killer went to Texas
As she moldered in her grave

If there's a lesson to be learned
It's that life is seldom fair
And sometimes justice is delayed
Until we face the perfect judge, waiting over there

HARD MAN

There was a hardness
built into this man,
laid brick on brick
by the harsh conditions
of frontier life.

Born into a family
of Kansas sodbusters,
always one calamity
away from starvation,
he faced a new threat
of early demise
at the age of fifteen,
when he was swept up
into the bowels of a war
in which he had no stake,
and no interest.

When the last shot was fired,
he navigated west,
finding a ready welcome
among young cowboys,
and fell in working the great
longhorn cattle drives;
another hazardous enterprise,
but one where hardness
counted as an asset,
and a short life
was the common expectation.

But now, years later,
having sidestepped
the Grim Reaper,
life, nevertheless,

JUST PASSIN' THRU

had taken its toll
on the hard man;
sun baked gullies
marked his face as one

in long partnership
with wind and sun,
and his clothes hung loosely
on his diminished frame.
Some teeth
had abandoned him,
and his hair had taken on
a frosty appearance
and a lower count.

But hard men
have no truck with the soft life
of bankers and ribbon clerks;
they do not retreat
to the comfort of rocking chairs
and feather beds.

He had always seen life
as a daily struggle
to survive another day,
and there was a hardness
built into this man,
laid brick on brick
by the harsh conditions
of frontier life.
The only thing
he knew he couldn't overcome
was the force of time.

BY THE BITTERROOT

He was a mongrel dog
His blood as mixed
And uncertain as my own
Perhaps that was what
Drew him to me
And I to him

He appeared
One twilight evening
In a tree line
Near my night camp
Where he watched
As I dressed out a wild turkey
For my supper

He came in slowly
Not afraid
But with the caution
Inbred in wild creatures
Came close enough
To feel the heat
Far enough away
To ensure his safety

He watched me
Through the eyes
Of a survivor
A creature who knew
Both the beauty
And the savagery
Of this untamed country

We shared the turkey
The warmth of the campfire

JUST PASSIN' THRU

And a night of sleep
Made pleasant
By the music
Of the Bitterroot River

Washing over rocks
Worn smooth
As the water itself
When I awoke
He was not there
But appeared again
As I stepped up
Into the saddle

He followed
Throughout the day
And kept easy pace
With my horse

And thus began
Our companionship
Our friendship
And our journey

If asked I would not
Have claimed ownership
Of this mongrel dog
We were two creatures
Of uncertain blood
Few expectations
And no fixed destination
We shared the road
And the campfire
And life

He was born a hunter
And often brought game

T C CARTER

To the fire
The rivers ran thick
With fish
And we dined on the bounty
Of nature

I traded skins
For shells and coffee

And other staples
He would never
Come into a town
But was always waiting
When I rode out

Sometimes he went away
For several days at a time
Having caught the scent
Of a female
In need of a mate
To insure the blood of life
Was not staunched

But he knew my scent
As well as he knew his own
And that remarkable gift
Always put him by my side
Once more

In all our years together
He had never become
A dog to be petted
He set boundaries
And I respected them

We saw the wonders
Of God's great western

JUST PASSIN' THRU

Creation
Together
But time was winding down
Our adventure

After all of time and travels
We found ourselves
In the same Montana valley
Of the Bitterroot Mountains
And made camp
In the same spot
Where I first saw him
Watching from the tree line

We shared wild turkey
Once again
And it seemed as if
We had never left
This cradle in the earth

I had settled down
Into my bedroll
When I felt the breath
Of the mongrel dog
On my face
He sank down
And rested his head
On my shoulder

I touched my hand
To his head
And felt his hair
For the first time
Stroked his head
As we drifted off to sleep
Warmed by the camp fire
And each other

T C CARTER

A night made pleasant
By the music
Of the Bitterroot River
Washing over rocks
Worn smooth
As the water itself

THE OLD COWPUNCHER

I'm just an old cowpuncher
somewheres north of my prime,
just a-waitin' fer Jesus
to tally up my time.

I've done my last round-up,
and rode my last trail,
spent my last night
in some dirty old jail.

Oh, I never was mean
and I wouldn't start a fight,
but I refused to be wrong
when I knew I was right.

And if push come to shove,
I'd still be mighty game,
but I'm telling you, son,
it wouldn't be the same,

'cause I'm slow as molasses,
and stiff as a post
and can't keep a reck'nin.
on what I have lost,

but I don't owe a peso
to nary a man,
and I'll pull my own weight
fer as long as I can,

so I'll stay at headquarters
and cook for the hands,
fer as long as they'll have me,
and as long as I can.

LAST THOUGHTS

The old cowpuncher tried to sit up
But he couldn't even lift his head
The thought that flashed a'crost his mind
Was, could it be I'm lying dead

When he'd stretched out on his bedroll
Last night at the close of day
He was too tired to even think
And way too tired to pray

He could hear the boys shuffling 'round
Gittin' ready fer the day
It would be another long one
Collecting puncher's pay

The sounds were all familiar
Part of life's music that he knew
He wanted to rise and play his part
With the rest of the waddie crew

But he could not make a move
His body was still as stone
He'd never been this helpless
Never felt quite so alone

His thoughts wandered back in time
To his younger days
When all the world seemed newly born
And he gave God His rightful praise

He'd been there when there was buffalo
Fer as the eye could see
And Injuns roaming all the west
Living wild and free

JUST PASSIN' THRU

He'd seen the valleys rich in grass
Standing four foot tall
Canyons colored bright as rainbows
That cradled waterfalls

At night the sky glowed with stars
That almost touched the ground
And drew marks across the heavens
That never made a sound

When the sun broke the grip of night
He remembered big skies clear and blue
Puffy clouds floating by
Passing slowly through

Once he'd been out where the redwoods
Dwarfed every living thing
And listened to the symphony
When the birds began to sing

He'd played cards with Wyatt Earp one time
Won sixteen dollars off'n him
When he left Wyatt shook his hand
And said, thanks fer coming in

He'd pushed cattle up the Chislom trail
Been in cowboy towns all about
Fell in love in Wichita
But she had turned him out

He'd gone from Texas up to Abilene
And never saw a fence
Never passed a built-up town
Or a sodbuster's settlement

He'd seen the railroad coming

T C CARTER

Tracks being laid from west and east
And he knew this wild, wild country
Would be devoured by the beast

But he had seen the big wild west
When it was clean and pure as gold
And helped to write the cowboy story
If the story would be told

Now the boys are looking at him
And calling out his name
Wondering if he was asleep
Or maybe come up lame

He thought, rein it in there fellers
There's a bright light that I see
It's purer than the brightest sun
And somebody's calling me

I'll have to be a' leaving now
Boys, I wish you all the best of luck
I've rode the wild mustang of life
And boys...looks like I've just been bucked

MONTANA COWBOY

I've been a cowboy most all my days,
I hail from out Montana way.
Onest in a while I'll run into
some old puncher that I always knew.

I'll pound his back and pump his hand;
we reminisce about old friends,
and back and forth we'll swap some words
the other man might not have heard.

A lot of things can pass us by
out here beneath Montana sky,
but the life the cowboy choses
gives him more than what he loses.

The town life don't fit the cowboy;
too many folks, too many rules,
too many card sharks and painted ladies,
too many drunks, too many fools.

But there's honest work with honest men
and freedom on the open plain;
if I could go back to my youth
I'd choose the cowboy life again.

I've been a cowboy most all my days,
I hail from out Montana way.
I've summed life up in some few words,
but said some more than I meant to say.

WYATT EARP

We buried Wyatt Earp today
Up on a grassy knoll
Here in Colma, California
Where he had gotten old

His years numbered eighty-one
His friends much more than that
Many came to see him off
Some cried just where they sat

Those grey and stooped old men
Who knew him long ago
When the west was truly wild
A place where legends grow

They huddled in long overcoats
To turn the wind away
And had their hats pulled down tight
On that cold January day

I could see it in their distant gaze
As they thought back to the past
To the times, now just a memory
Times that could not last

I knew they were reliving
Some event that they held dear
Something from their younger days
Replaying crystal clear

Perhaps they thought of Wyatt
And his even disposition
Or the things he said he'd like to do
That never saw fruition

JUST PASSIN' THRU

Thirty seconds at the O.K.
Was all the time it took
To make his reputation
And put him in the history books

Some had seen that gunfight
That's still talked about today
Some knew him from Dodge City
And up Nome, Alaska way

But just like men everywhere
There was much they never shared
They depended on their actions
To show how much they cared

The shadows of the past
Swept over wrinkled brows
And the things they had meant to say
Would have to be said now

I could see their lips moving
As they said their last good-byes
And said the things 'til now unsaid
As tears fell from their eyes

LET ME RIDE

Boys, help me to the saddle
Don't leave me here in town
Let me ride out to the prairie
Let that be the place I'm found

If it's time to join my pardners
If it's time for me to die
Let me ride out to the prairie
Let me ride up to the sky

I don't need no fancy doings
I don't need a lot of fuss
Let me ride out to the prairie
While I sing In God I Trust

All my life I've been a cowboy
And a good one; I've been true
To my God up there in heaven
And the cowboys that I knew

I've tried to live the good book
I've tried to take a stand
And where it counts
And when it counts
I think I've made a hand

Boys, help me to the saddle
I want to hear the coyote call
Let me ride out to the prairie
You can plant me where I fall

I want to once more see the sunset
Shining on a sea of grass
And breathe the air of freedom

JUST PASSIN' THRU

For as long as I can last

So, boys, help me to the saddle
Don't leave me here in town
Let me ride out to the prairie
Let that be the place I'm found

SHAKESPEARE

That Shakespeare feller,
he shore did write
some fancy words,
purdiest ones I reckon
that I ever heard.

Trail boss reads us cowboys
some few pages
ever' night
by campfire light,
so the story comes to us
in stages.

Someday I think
it would be fittin'
if we could buck out
one whole story
in jest one sittin'.

THE FARMER'S SON

My dear old pappy thought
That I was just a wee bit strange
To want to leave those cotton fields
And ply the open range

For he was wedded to the land
And planting cotton in a row
And praying for the rain to come
To make the cotton grow

But we had heard about the cowboys
From a stranger passing through
And he swore that all he told to us
Could be certified as true

He said that when they'd ride to town
With jingle in their jeans
They'd spend it all or lose it all
Like they were men of means

You could hear their jolly laughter
And the ribald way they talked
And the music of their rusty spurs
Wherever they would walk

And smoke would drift into the street
From roll-your-owns and cheap cigars
And whiskey flowed by bucket loads
Across the well-worn bar

Sometimes there'd be some gunshots
Let loose upon the air
Just to let the town observers
Know they didn't have a care

T C CARTER

But oft-times hot lead flying
Was meant to kill a man
For law was loosely exercised
In that raw-boned frontier land

And when the night was fully wasted
And the dawn was breaking through
The gathered up and saddled up
And away the cowboys flew

They left behind shotgun saloons
And painted ladies of the night
And every nickel in their jeans
Had been spent on town delights

Back to work they would ride
These princes of the plains
These buccaneers of longhorn steers
These riders of the purple sage

Well, this story got me dreaming
As I lay there on my bed
And I was riding with the cowboys
On the trail inside my head

In another year I'd be sixteen
Time to stand up as a man
And figure out exactly how
To carry out my plan

But for now I'd rise up every day
and work hard at my chores
And help my pa with all my strength
For just one season more

Then some fine morn

JUST PASSIN' THRU

On some fine day
I'll kiss my ma, hug my pa
And by first light be on my way

Will the cowboy life suit me
There's just one way to tell
And that's to lay aside all doubt
And plant myself on the western trail

LOVING LIES

Long time since he'd been home.
Called Mama from Tucson.
She didn't know he'd been in jail,
and he didn't tell her.
Last she knew he was still rodeoing,
but that come to an end two years ago.
He was gettin' by, making ends meet,
'till that old bull busted him up so bad.
Now he weren't much good for nothing.
Couldn't say he was homesick really,
but he was sick.
Didn't tell her that neither.

She answered on the first ring.
He knew she was sittin' in that old
recliner chair
with a little mongrel dog on her lap,
and a cold coffee cup on the side table.
He could hear the television
in the background,
tuned to the weather channel.
She said Papa was out back
piddling with something in the shed.
She'd call him but he was deaf
as a tree stump
and she couldn't walk down
that rough old path anymore.
But, no, no, he was doing fine,
she was doing fine,
long as they remembered
to take their medications
and didn't eat too much fatty foods.

He knew that wasn't true.

JUST PASSIN' THRU

Nobody there was doing fine
since the cotton mills shut down.
He knew their monthly check
always had to be stretched thin.

Did he think he could be home
for her birthday this August the tenth?
He'd try but that was a busy rodeo month.
She wished he could
just come on back home to live.
He said he did too,
but that was another thing
that wasn't true.
He couldn't show up there
broke and sick
with nothing to show
for the last seven years.
She couldn't admit there was no future
for him there anyway,
or tell him that she spent most days worried
about what lay in front of her and Papa.

The truth of life was a weight neither of them
was able or willing to shoulder,
so they told each other loving lies,
for a few more minutes,
before they let the line,
go silent.

WHAT COWBOYS DO

Dark clouds forming in the western sky
Smell of rain is on the wind
Cattle bawl and mill about
Caught up in the pen

Slickers on, buttoned tight
To keep the cowboys dry
'Cause sure as hell the rain will fall
From that blackened sky

Already in the saddle they eat what grub they can
'Cause if them bovines spook and run
There's no way to tell a'tall
When they might eat ag'in

Thunder rolls acros't the boiling sky
Like cannon balls acros't a wooden floor
And lightening slashes through the mass
And lights up the soggy core

A bolt of golden lightning strikes a piñon tree
And turns its light to fire
Cattle, wild- eyed and terrified
Stampede as one from the funeral pyre

The water breaks in mother sky
And floods down on the plain
The race is on to save the herd
In the driving rain

The storm plays out it's symphony
From first note to its last
And soon enough the sun breaks through
As the storm has passed

JUST PASSIN' THRU

But now it's two days in the gather
Cattle tired, men and horses too
A few winks of saddle sleep, not much to eat
But we don't quit until we're through

You might say we're crazy
And we might agree it's true
But the way we see the life we live
It's just what cowboys do

CROSSING OVER

The years had gone by quickly
He'd grown old out on the trail
But he would make this last drive
In that he would not fail

He thought back to his first time
On that trail to Abilene
Riding over countryside
That he had never seen

He'd slept beneath the big sky
And gazed up at the starry lights
Glowing like ten thousand angels
To soften the black of night

He'd worked and joked with cowboys
And made some right good friends
But now he'd played his string out
And was coming to the end

Doc said it was a tumor
Too big to cut it out
It was time to take a look
At what his life was all about

Well, it had been a simple life
He'd worked to earn his keep
He'd tried to live by the holy book
'Cause what you sow is what you reap

He believed all that God had said
And he knew His only Son
He figured God would surely say
His spurs were fairly won

JUST PASSIN' THRU

He didn't have much to leave
Behind when he was gone
Mostly just his cowboy tack
And his big strawberry roan

But he'd made up a paper
The trail boss had it now
He'd carry out the final wishes
Boss had took a solemn vow

He thought he'd been a good man
That is, as far as good men go
He'd been fair in all his dealings
His word was his bond, don't ya know

He thought he'd leave behind him
A name that settled well
On the tongues of men and angels
If his story they would tell

And so he was reconciled
To the trail he had to ride
It was what he had to do
To cross the great divide

DOC HOLLIDAY'S ACCOUNTING

Being of relatively sound mind
but rapidly failing body
I have determined to execute
a brief accounting of my life
with the assistance
of my saintly nurse
Sister Rebecca
of the order of the Sisters
of Mercy

She comes here
to the Hotel Glenwood
twice a day
to attend to my needs
and has agreed to transcribe
my words

I have ceased availing myself
of the sulfur vapors
of the famous Yampah Hot Springs
as I have seen no help or cure
forthcoming
and I have grown too weak
to make the effort

My dearly beloved Mother perished
when I was but a lad of fifteen years
from this scourge of tuberculosis
that has ravaged me

She and my father
provided a genteel upbringing
for me in Griffin, Georgia
and I studied for a career

JUST PASSIN' THRU

in the field of dentistry
but when I became ill
I traveled west hoping a different climate
would aid my condition
I became proficient in the use
of firearms
and skillful in the art of gambling
I discovered the medicinal qualities
of consuming generous prescriptions
of whiskey

This chronicle is not meant
to substitute for a last will and testament
as I have nothing left
to bequeath to anyone
I have no family left
that I am aware of
and since my departure from
Tombstone, Arizona
have had no contact
with my one-time traveling companion
and lover, Kate Horony
widely known as Big Nose Kate

There have been many tales
of my murderous adventures
in the west
many of which I fabricated myself
for the purpose of instilling fear
in other men
It proved to be a useful tool
when unpleasant disagreements
had to be settled

Although I have engaged in a number
of altercations involving the employment
of gunplay

T C CARTER

I had never killed a man
until the day I shot and killed
Tom McLaury
near the O.K. corral
Although there is some contention
and uncertainty in the matter

I believe it was my bullet
that dispatched his brother
Frank McLaury, as well

I was compliant
in the killing of other men
as I abetted Wyatt Earp
in raining down vengeance
on the cowboys
who assassinated his brother
Morgan
and maimed brother
Virgil

Wyatt Earp was my friend
the only one who ever stood
solidly with me
and the only man
I would have given my life for
We said our last goodbye
before I came here
to Glenwood Springs, Colorado
I wanted our parting to take place
while I was still able
to care for myself
not in a place such as this
where the grim reaper occupies
every shadow

At my request

JUST PASSIN' THRU

Wyatt agreed not to make any attempt
to see me again
We both knew what the weight
of that agreement meant

It seems there has been
considerable attention
given to the gunfight in Tombstone
by the pulp fiction writers
and others attempting to profit

in some way
But, I expect that will pass in time
and Wyatt and I
will be forgotten
along with the Clantons
and the McLaurys
and others on the edges
of what the public has come to know
as gunfight at the O.K. corral

Perhaps it's best that way

END OF TRAIL

Come now, boys, gather 'round,
and get your pay.
Before you do I'd like to say,
I never thought I'd see the day
when cattle drives would not stay.

But here we are, boys, end of trail;
you'll draw your pay, collect your mail,
drink too much and feel like hell,
but mark this, boys, and mark it well,
cowboys will never go away.

HELL FAR', BOYS

Hell far', boys, ain't much ya can say
fer 'a old cowpoke
been busted up much as this 'un
I lost track 'a broke bones
long time ago

Hell far', boys, got more stitches
in me than a ready made
suit 'a clothes

Pass 'at thar jug over here, Chester
Onley'est medicine 'at cuts
the pain these days
Oh, I ain't complainin' none

Hell far', boys, most 'a the punchers
I rode with has already cashed thar chips in
Least I'm still on the grassy side 'a the dirt

Back in sebney-nine Charlie Tate
got hisself up under a herd
'a stampedin' longhorns
couple 'a years later
Woodrow Peabody dropped dead
in a bawdy house up in Cheyenne
Gus Wilson shot dead in Abilene
heard it was a cancer
what kilt J.J. Fletcher

Hell far', boys, I could go on and on
but most 'a y'all is too young
to 'a knowed them fellers

While you got a'holt of that jug, Bill

T C CARTER

pour me another snort
if you've a mind to
Goes down mean, don't it

But hell far', boys, listen here
them fellers is gone on t' meet thar maker
and they was all good hands
down to a man
so I 'spect they got hired on up yonder
no worries 'bout them

Oh…hell far', boys, I should 'a said sumpin'
'bout old Haywood Montgomery
Some 'a y'all might 'a heard 'a Haywood
used t' ride fer the T bar T ?

Dead?….hell far', boys
Naw, it's worse 'n that
he got hisself mixed up inta politics

MOVING ON

Well boys we've got the herd
Up here to Wichita ones't ag'in
Trail boss is over yonder
A'settlin' up by the cattle pens

And we're milling 'round and jawing
Waitin' to draw our puncher's pay
And telling all we aim to do
Fer the next handful of days

But boys I won't be joinin' in
The cow trail life is shrinkin' down
Gittin' to be too many fences
Too many tracks, too many towns

So boys I'm gonna be moving on
They say Montana is the place to be
Fer men who crave the open space
And hanker to be free

So I'm a' headin' up the northwest trail
It's a mighty long way to go
I aim to settle in somewhere
Before the winters' blowing snow

Now if any of you bold cow punchers
Sees things the same way that I do
You're welcome to ride along with me
And I'd be proud to ride with you

They say the big sky country
Ain't fer men what's lacking grit
But them what's cut from rawhide and river rock
And never learnt the meanin' of "quit"

T C CARTER

So ride with me, boys
If ya think you've a mind to
Don't wait 'till work is plumb run out
And there ain't a thing that you can do

Boys, we've rolled the dice before
When we left the south behind
And come to Texas green as grass
With cow punching on our minds

But now it's time we was moving on
We ain't the kind to settle down
Cain't be a bunkhouse cowboy
And wouldn't last a month in town

So it's done and settled, boys
Here comes boss man with our pay
We'll be headin' to Montana
By the middle of the day

THE PARK

The old man sat on a park bench
Watching life go by
And thinking some on better days
When he was young and spry

He had lived his life as a cowboy
But there's no call for trail hands now
That way of life was swept away
By railroads and the farmer's plow

But he was one of them rawhide fellers
Whose hearts called them to the west
To drive cattle towards the north star
Each one trying to do his best

He had been a part of something special
That won't come around another day
That slice of life you hope to keep
That never seems to stay

Oh, they were heady days
And those were princely men
That's what he thought of them
And, it's what they thought of him

But now he's feeding peanuts
To pigeons in the park
Instead of being on the range
Where he had made his mark

No sense in being sorry
That's just the way life goes
How the time slips by...so fast
I guess nobody knows

T C CARTER

But this is what it's come to
After years out on the range
Sitting in a city park
Out of place and feeling strange

Don't see as many horses
Now they've got these motor cars
And lights at night up on a pole
That makes it hard to see the stars

City folks thinks it's better
Living squeezed up in some town
But you'll never find an old cowboy
Who doesn't long to hear the sounds

Of a herd of longhorns moving north
The coyotes' song up in the hills
The talks around the campfires
All these things remembered still

But life has many faces
Nothing seems to stay the same
He would adapt to his new life
And accept things the way they came

He'd be satisfied with autumn days
Sudden showers in the spring
Horizons topped by rainbows
And sweet memories they bring

He'd be a friend to the pigeons
Giving 'em peanuts on the grass
And never worry about tomorrow
Or be too sad about the past

He'd remember what his paw had said

JUST PASSIN' THRU

Years ago when they said goodbye
Always do what's right and honest, son
And never let 'em see you cry

THINGS REMEMBERED

Well, it got to the place where I couldn't ride
leastwise, not to make much of a show
so I picked up pencil and paper
and wrote 'bout the rodeo

I wrote 'bout the open prairies
and cattle drives when I was young
'bout the ladies that I've loved
and the songs that I've sung

'Bout the Llano Estacado
where it's flat as a dollar bill
and many a man has lost his way
looking for tree or hill

I wrote 'bout the old-time lawmen
no braver men t' be found
not many left to tell their tales
most rest below the ground

I wrote 'bout the railroads coming
'bout the buffalo I've seen run
'bout the nights with stars down to the ground
and days full of blazing sun

And I wrote some 'bout the Indians
and the raw deal come their way
hard things to write about
hard things to say

I wrote 'bout all the good old boys
left behind in shallow graves
with nothing to mark that lonely spot
'cept maybe a stone or stave

113

JUST PASSIN' THRU

But if fair and square is what yer' looking for
I hate to bust yer' bubble
life has got its good side
but it's also filled with trouble

But I've wrote it down the way I see it
with no regrets or blame to lay
good and bad, I told it all
'cause that's the cowboy way

So if our trails by chance should cross
and you hanker to hear a tale or two
just ask 'bout things remembered
and I'll pass you on a few

OLD TIMER

It seems I tend to write about
Things coming to an end
About me and fellers like me
On the backside of the bend

I've lately took to saying
I've been around as long as dirt
Sometimes I think it's funny
Other times it kind 'a hurts

Rain's been thin and seldom
Fer three years in a row
Ponds are mostly dried up
And the grass cain't hardly grow

Ain't got no cattle now to feed
'Cept a milk cow in the yard
Got a horse I hardly ever ride
Seems the effort's just too hard

The bunkhouse, well, it's empty
Had to let the cowboys go
The market went to pieces
Price of cattle too dang low

The wife, she keeps some laying hens
And I'd have eggs most every day
But Doc says my cholesterol
Would surely make me pay

But I reckon we been lucky
The banker's loan is paid in full
And the real estate developers
Come around to shoot the bull

115

JUST PASSIN' THRU

I'm not of a mind to sell the place
We worked too hard to make it go
But what the future holds fer us
There ain't no way to know

We put away a little savings
It ain't much, it won't last long
But maybe we can stretch it out
And stay where we belong

Oh, I'll keep on a' writing
My poems and songs and such
Even though it's getting harder
To think of very much

I'll write some more about my friends
Been thinking some on Grady Sloan
A top hand back in better days
Now he's old and lives alone

Then there's Big Ben Riley
Got that spread just north of me
Last I heard he was still there
I ought to ride up there and see

Lefty Slocum, Jacob Morgan
Them and others grown old now
But they lived some cowpunch stories
That need to be preserved somehow

I could write about the young 'uns
But they've all moved away to towns
And I cain't think of what I'd write
'Bout folks that ain't around

PLAIN AND SIMPLE

There's fellers that write
plain and simple,
in language that's well understood
by the young and the old,
the meek and the bold,
and even the bad and the good.

These cowboy word wranglers
ain't stupid, some got a college degree;
but I never had too much schooling,
so the top of the class would not include me.

I have lived on the rough edges of life
where poor folks do the best that they can,
and the things that they want
and the things that they need
are seldom acquired according to plan.

I's raised in a ramshackle shanty
on forty acres of dust,
learnin' the art of survival
and looking for something in life
I could trust.

Then I found out, when I was all growd up,
with life pert near spent in the grind,
that the living of life,
and the joy and the strife
was puttin' words I could write in my mind.

Now, I sure ain't the best, fer sure ain't the worst,
I guess in between is about where I'd fit
and when I was knocked down, I always got up,
not looking at the backside, but gittin' on with it.

JUST PASSIN' THRU

Ya know, I never did finish in first place,
but I dang sure never finished up last;
and I think, when I try to consider my stories,
most of them come from my life in the past.

CLOSING PRAYER

Dear Lord, I've rode my last round-up
I'm a'hangin' up my spurs today
I'm sad that it's come to this
But I cain't see no other way

I ain't a young man anymore
My hair's gone thin and grey
Cain't see the way I used t' see
Or always hear what others say

And gittin' in the saddle now
Has become a painful chore
The rhumetiz, it's gittin' worse
Keeps me stiff and sore

But I'm grateful fer the life I've had
The cowboys that I've known
Why, I've been working from the saddle
Since I was 'bout half grown

And the life, it ain't been easy
Its had its ups and downs
But I wouldn't trade one minute
Fer all the easy jobs in town

It was outdoor life I wanted
Independence was my need
Pappy thought I'd till the sod
But I gave that thought no heed

I never had much chance at church
Sittin' in a wooden pew
Singing songs with other folks
Most times it's been just me and You

119

JUST PASSIN' THRU

And, Lord, I've had yer good book
With me all my many days
Ain't nearly got her bucked out
Trying to figger out yer ways

But as near as I can figger
And I know I ain't too smart
It ain't as much about the head
As it is about the heart

Now book learnin', it's a good thing
Long as it ain't overdone
Ya gotta leave some room fer living life
And having a little fun

It seems t' me the cowboy creed
Ain't too far off the mark
Of what You had in mind fer man
To shine some light into the dark

So, with Jesus as my trail boss
And You headin' up the rodeo
I got a heap of curiosity
To find out where we're gonna go

So,if you'll just point the way, Lord
I'll follow best way that I can
I might be done with round-ups
But I'm still ridin' fer the brand

AMEN

COWBOY CHRISTMAS

It was the night before Christmas, and out on the prairie
I was thinking 'bout Jesus and Joseph and Mary,
and what it all meant, that babe on the hay;
a gift to the world that was born the next day.

Now the cattle were all bedded down for the night,
and the stars in the sky were shining so bright,
while I on my horse, under my hat,
was feeling right drowsy and needin' a nap,

when out in the distance I heard a faint clatter
as I sang to the cattle so they wouldn't scatter.
I kept my eyes peeled out towards the new sound
to see what it was that was coming around.

The moon and the stars gave just enough light
to make it look halfway between daytime and night,
and all of a sudden I saw it real clear;
a Conestoga wagon was coming up near.

The driver was aged, his beard long and gray
and I knew in a moment he'd come a long way,
but his horses were strong and up to the chore
of pulling that wagon for many miles more.

He said, hup Jake, on Charger, step up Kaleen,
giddy-up Lightning, pull now, my team.
Four beauties they were, fourteen hands high;
no finer team has ever filled my green eyes.

Then he pulled up the team a-ways out from the camp
and back in the wagon came a light from a lamp,
and in just a few minutes he came out with a bound
and set a big sack of stuff down on the ground.

JUST PASSIN' THRU

He was dressed in a coat made of buffalo hide
and looked like a cowboy ready to ride,
but he scooped up his sack, on his shoulder it went
and I was startin' to figure out just what it all meant.

His eyes had a shine like the stars up above
and his ruddy old face you just had to love,
for his smile was as big and as broad as an axe
as he marched toward the camp with his big, bulging sack

Well, the cowboys were sleeping and snoring a tune
as they lay in their bedrolls beneath the full moon,
and the jolly old cowboy was stepping real light
and leaving gifts by the snoozers on that Christmas Eve
night.

Now this is the thing I ain't figgered out yet:
the gifts were wrapped up in paper from the North Pole
Gazette
and when I rode in for coffee, right there plain to see
was a newspaper package addressed, yep, to me.

Well, that night he was gone as quick as he came
and I wish I could say what I think is his name,
and you might be thinking the same thing as me
but then, I think again, how can such a thing be?

But up on his wagon with a word to his team
he had faded away like a sweet Christmas dream,
and as he rode out of sight I heard his voice on the wind,
MERRY CHRISTMAS TO ALL OF MY COWPUNCHING
FRIENDS.

FORECLOSED

In the silvery pre-dawn light,
the world in silhouette,
he gazes across the pasture,
and rolls a Bull Durham cigarette.

Steam rises from his thermos cup,
the metal warming his finger tips
as he tries to come to grips
with the ranch going belly up.

He sees the absent horses,
no longer his,
in the pasture of his mind,
fallen to the auctioneer's hammer;
they could have left Caesar behind,

past his prime, he was retired,
love alone holding his place
in the pasture and paddock.
He deserves better
than what he'll receive
in this world of hard knocks.

A last sip of coffee,
he field-strips the cigarette,
gets in his truck,
leaving the roots of his heart
braided into Mother Earth,
and drives away,
with his sadness.

About the Author
T.C. Carter came to the world of poetry late in his life but has written
extensively for more than a decade. His subjects have ranged over
a wide variety of subjects, including works focused on the military,
cowboy life, experiences growing up in the south of the nineteen-
fifties and other areas of life. His first published book "Just Passin'
Thru" is a collection from his cowboy creations. He was born in
Danville, Virginia, lived much of his life in the west, and is retired in
North Carolina with his wife, Judy.

www.ingramcontent.com/pod-product-compliance
Lightning Source LLC
Chambersburg PA
CBHW070724130626
46553CB00005B/2132